AF379714

This book is a work of fiction designed to provide helpful information on the subjects discussed. Effort has been made to ensure that this information is accurate and complete, however, this book is not meant to be used, nor should it be used, to diagnose or treat any medical condition. For diagnosis or treatment of any medical problem, consult your own physician. The publisher and author are not responsible for any specific health or allergy needs that may require medical supervision and are not liable for any damages or negative consequences from any treatment, action, application or preparation, to any person reading or following the information in this book.

The Cookie

A story of friendship and food allergy

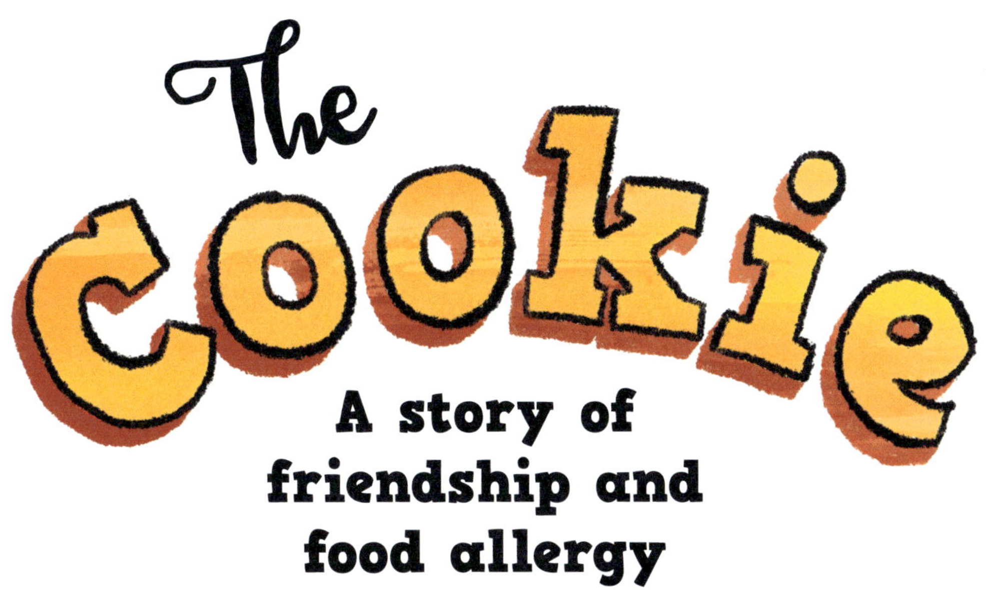

Written and illustrated by
Kath Grimshaw

For my Laurie,
who has learned to go without
and, in doing so, has gained empathy,
kindness and fortitude

Foreword

I am a consultant in Paediatric Allergy and Immunology.
When Kath asked me to look over *The Cookie* as an expert
reader, I offered to write a foreword for the book.

The Cookie helps to explain allergies in a simple and
comprehensive way and to teach young children with a
food allergy how to navigate the world safely. It looks at the
impact of an allergy on their lives at school and at home
and addresses important issues of bullying and teasing.

Food allergies affect 3-6% of children in the developed world.
That's one child in every classroom. This book is a great
introduction to allergies for young children and I would
recommend it in the classroom and for families who have
just received an allergy diagnosis. It is vital that children
with allergies feel accepted and safe and the key to that is
empathy and understanding.

Dr Helen Brough

Laurie and Lewis were best friends.

They got their
first teeth together,

took their first
steps together,

said their first
words together.

Lewis and Laurie loved:

trains,

Sometimes they fought over their toys.

They were told to

Laurie and Lewis were in the same class at school.

Laurie loved maths and Lewis loved art.

Lewis loved football

and Laurie loved tennis.

But they both loved **play time** the best.

One day, Laurie forgot his snack.
"Don't worry," said Lewis, "You can share my cookie."
He snapped it in half and gave some to his friend.

But when Laurie ate
the cookie, he began
to feel really bad.
His mouth felt spiky
and he was sick.

Lewis ran to
get the teacher.
The teacher
was worried
and called an
ambulance.

The ambulance came quickly.
It took Laurie to hospital.

The children were excited to see an ambulance but Lewis felt terrible. He was worried about his friend. He thought sharing was good, but now he wasn't so sure.

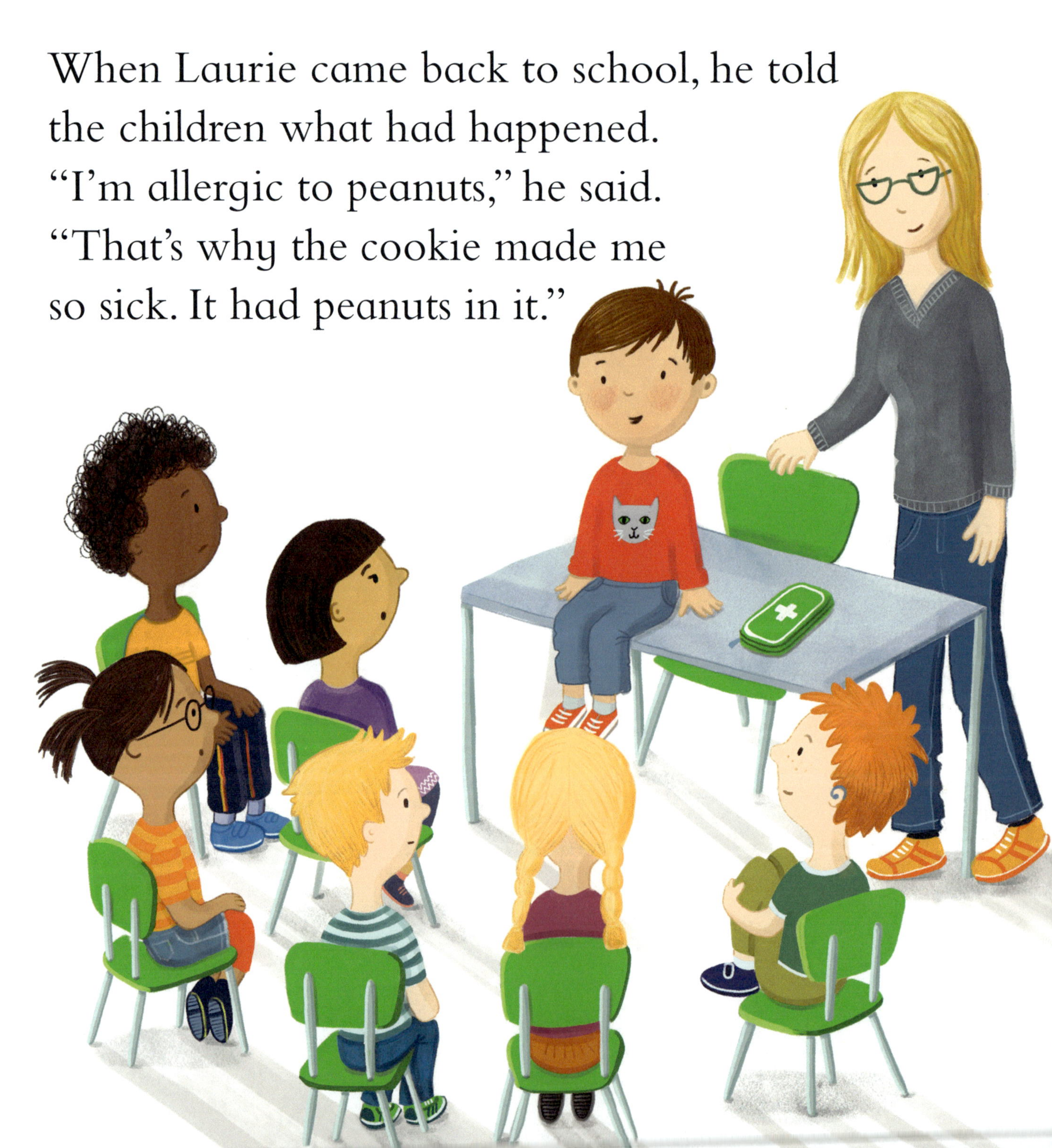

When Laurie came back to school, he told
the children what had happened.
"I'm allergic to peanuts," he said.
"That's why the cookie made me
so sick. It had peanuts in it."

"When I eat peanuts my body thinks they are attacking me so it fights back, which makes me very poorly."

Laurie said, "I have some new rules to keep me safe."

I can't ever eat peanuts, or even touch a peanut.

Peanut Butter

If I do eat some, or if I feel ill, I have to tell a teacher straight away.

I must check ingredients before eating anything.

And I'm not allowed to share food.

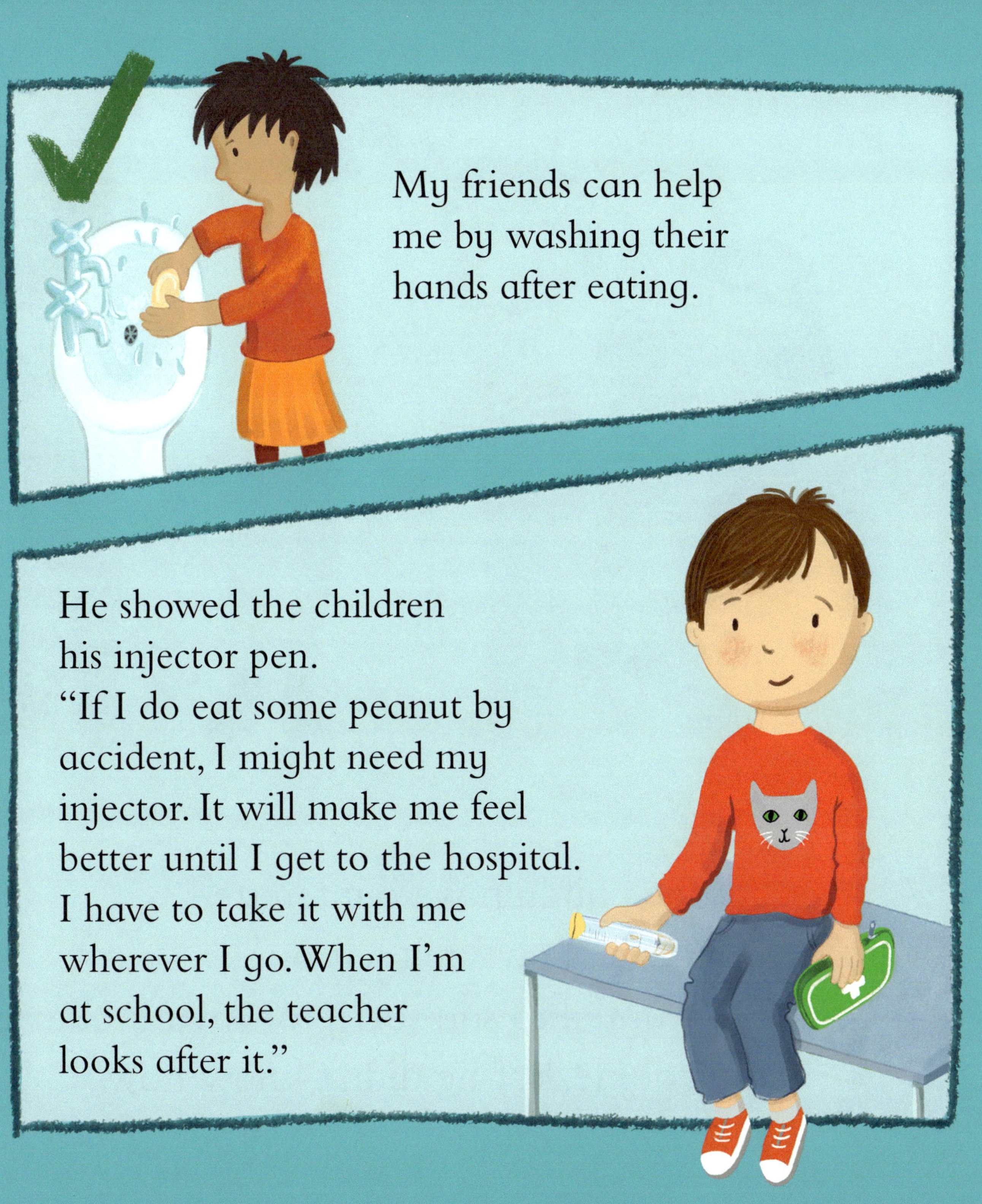

My friends can help me by washing their hands after eating.

He showed the children his injector pen.
"If I do eat some peanut by accident, I might need my injector. It will make me feel better until I get to the hospital. I have to take it with me wherever I go. When I'm at school, the teacher looks after it."

All the children were interested
in Laurie. Lewis felt left out.
He wanted to say sorry for giving Laurie
the cookie, but he didn't know how.

Laurie had lots of new friends now, so Lewis
made a new friend too. He was called Harry.

The next day, Laurie sat with Lewis and
Harry at lunch time.
"You'd better keep away – my snack bar
might have peanuts in it!" Harry laughed.
Lewis didn't think it was funny, but he wasn't
brave enough to tell Harry.

Harry was having a birthday party.
He invited nearly everyone.
"I'm not inviting Laurie because
I might have nuts on my cake!"
he said to Lewis.

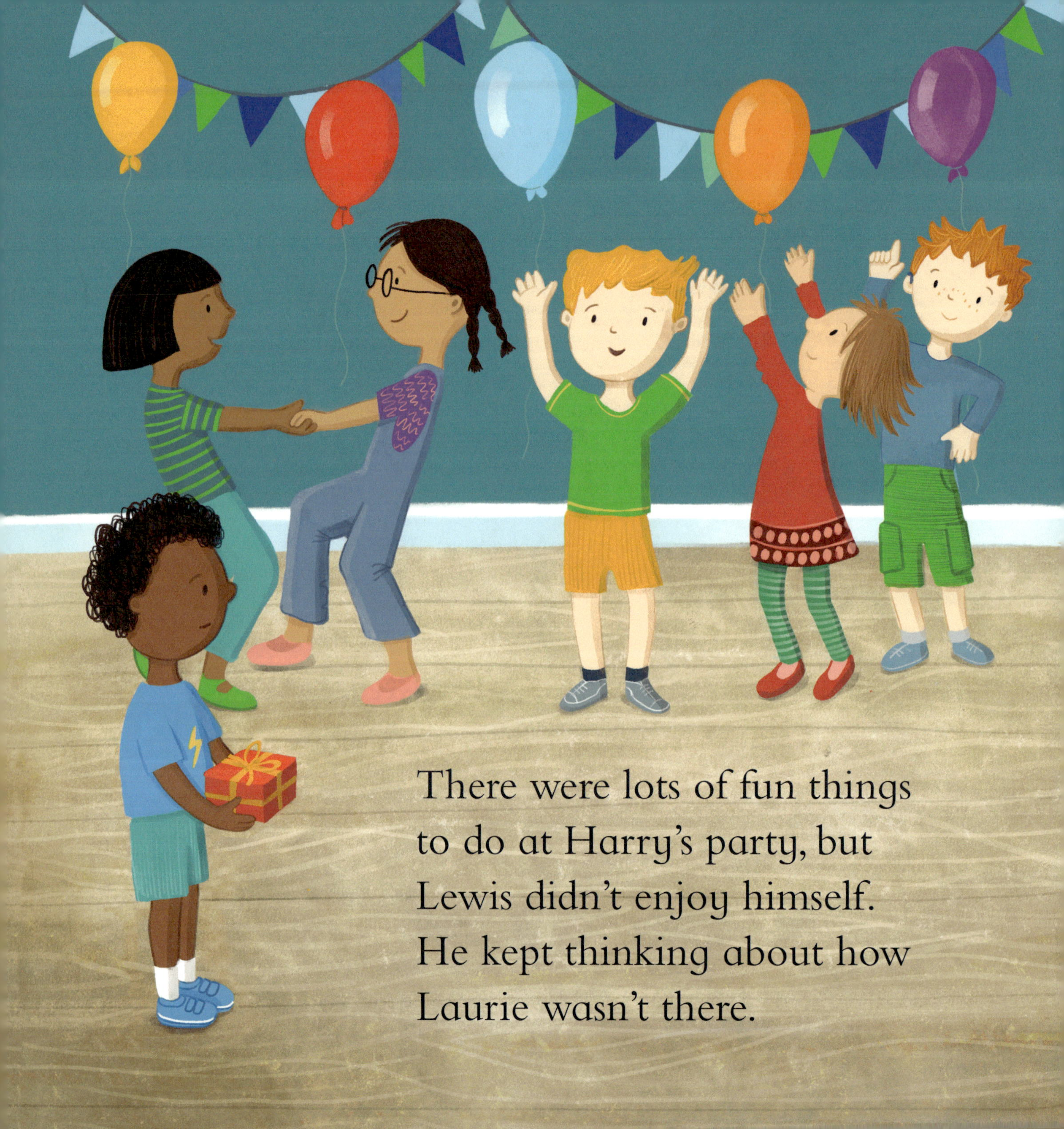

There were lots of fun things
to do at Harry's party, but
Lewis didn't enjoy himself.
He kept thinking about how
Laurie wasn't there.

When Lewis' dad picked him up, he asked
him what was wrong.
Lewis told his dad.
"Don't worry," said Dad, "I've got an idea."

Lewis and his dad made some special cookies.
They checked all the ingredients to make sure nothing
said **May Contain Peanuts,** and they wiped the
kitchen clean and used clean bowls before cooking.

Then they took
the cookies to
Laurie's house.

Lewis said, "I'm sorry I gave you
the cookie that made you ill."
"That's okay," said Laurie.
"You ran so fast to get help."

"I felt jealous because you were special, and
everyone wanted to be your friend," said Lewis.
"I don't want to be special," said Laurie.
"And I want to be **your** friend."

Laurie and Lewis were glad to be best friends again. They played all afternoon.

When it was Lewis' birthday,
he invited all the children in
the class. And he made sure
that all the party food was
nut-free, even the cake!

FOR PARENTS, TEACHERS AND CARERS

This book aims to teach children about allergies in a friendly and accessible way

THE KEY TEACHING POINTS IT ILLUSTRATES ARE:

Scenarios where food allergies have to be managed outside the home (e.g., school settings and birthday parties).

Outward symptoms and what happens to your body in an allergic reaction (see pull-out box).

An introduction to Epipens and other autoinjectors.

The importance of not sharing food.

The importance of telling a grown-up swiftly if you or your allergic friend feels ill.

The importance of checking labels for ingredients and avoiding risks of cross-contamination.

Allergy bullying can take place in different ways, including teasing and exclusion.

Kids with allergies don't want to feel different or 'special'.

Friends can make changes to be inclusive and help to keep each other safe.

* Epipen is one type of autoinjector. There are other types, such as Emerade and Jext. Follow the instructions for use.

Symptoms of an allergic reaction

Eyes
Itchy, watery.

Nose
Runny or stuffy nose, sneezing.

Lungs
Chest tightness, wheezing, trouble breathing.

Stomach
Nausea, vomiting, diarrhea.

Skin
Hives or skin rash.

Brain
Confused, anxious, sense of doom.

Mouth
Swollen tongue or lips, itchy mouth.

Heart
Dizziness, fainting, drop in blood pressure.

Skin
Flushed or pale skin.

A list of the most common allergens.

Peanuts

Celery

Dairy

Sesame

Egg

Lupin

Gluten

Tree Nuts

Soya

Shell Fish

Mustard

Crustacean

Fish

Sulphites

Look out for these ingredients when reading food labels.

ABOUT THE AUTHOR
AND ILLUSTRATOR

Hello, I'm Kath. My son Laurie was diagnosed with a peanut allergy at the age of three after a bite of his friend's peanut butter sandwich. Over the years, we have learned to adapt, check and avoid in order to keep Laurie safe, but we also try to make sure that he is not defined by his allergy.

One of the most challenging aspects of living with a food allergy is often the lack of awareness in other people. I wanted to write a story that helps to educate all children (and their parents, teachers and carers) about allergies but that is also, at heart, a tale of friendship and empathy.

I am a writer and illustrator and I live in Devon, UK, with my husband, two boys, three cats and a spaniel.

ACKNOWLEDGEMENTS

Thank you...

to Dr Helen Brough for her expertise and generosity

to Kath and Robbie for their editorial eagle eyes;

to all the people in the allergy community who have given me advice and encouragement;

to Ailia for being my first reader;

to Sam, who looks out for his little brother (mostly) uncomplainingly;

to Laurie's brilliant friends, who are inclusive and caring;

to Shaun, my double-checker;

and, of course, to Laurie for his endurance and cheerfulness when all around him are eating birthday cake.

Made in the USA
Monee, IL
07 July 2026

56550988R00024